Pupil's Book

GW00691995

3

Hopscotch

JENNIFER HEATH

Rubrics

English	My language
Chant	
Circle	
Draw	
Listen	
Look	
Make	
Match	
Number	
Play	
Read	
Say	
Sing	
Stick	
Talk	
Tick	
Watch	
Write	

Contents

Unit 1 My hobby

Riding a bike is a great hobby.

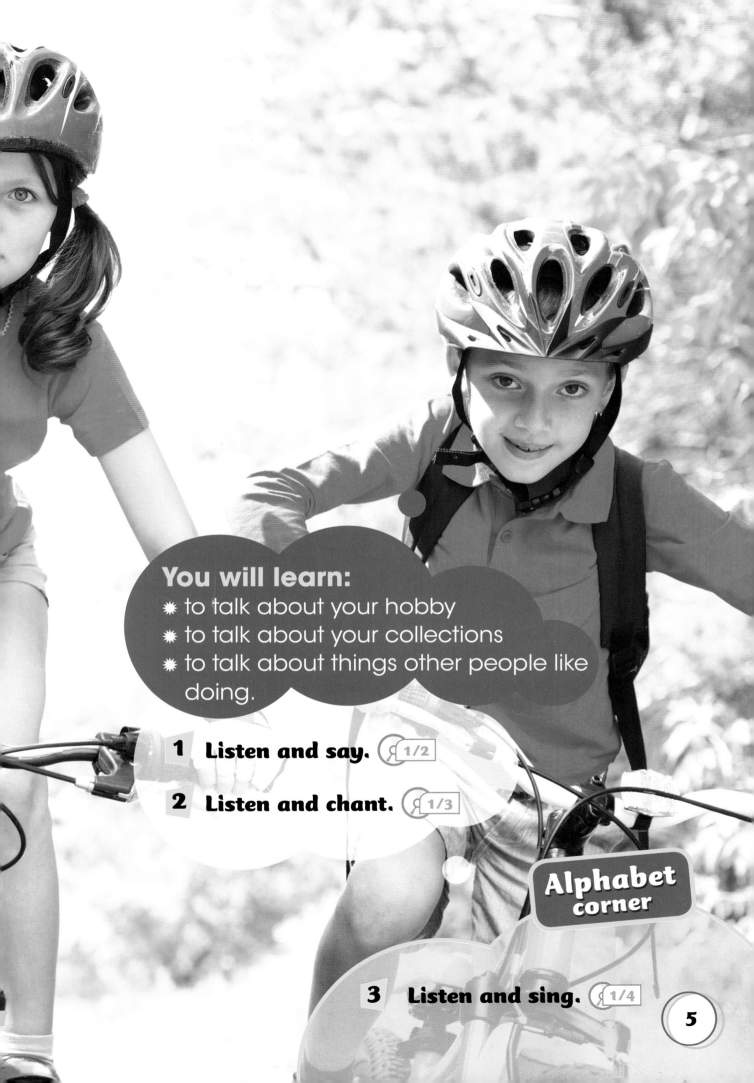

You will learn:
- ☀ to talk about your hobby
- ☀ to talk about your collections
- ☀ to talk about things other people like doing.

1 Listen and say. 1/2

2 Listen and chant. 1/3

Alphabet corner

3 Listen and sing. 1/4

5

I ride a horse.

Write the words and expressions in your language in the 'My language' column of the Word list at the end of the book.

> ride a horse   favourite   Let me …   take a photo
> do karate   Help!   play the piano
> write a story/write stories

1 Listen, say and play.

2 Listen, read and make.

Story corner

1 Pupils learn the new words and play the *Guessing Game*. ⟳TB
2 Pupils listen to the dialogue, follow the story and read the sentences. ⟳TB

3 Stick and read.

1

2

3

4

5

4 Write and read.

rides   does   writes   takes   plays

karate   stories   the piano   her horse   photos

1 Snap _____ .

2 Chatty _____ .

3 Kate _____ .

4 Honey _____ .

5 Fred _____ .

5 Listen and sing. 1/7

3 Pupils stick the correct sentences in the speech bubbles and read the sentences aloud.
4 Pupils complete the sentences about the characters using the words from the boxes and read them aloud.
5 Pupils listen to the song and sing all together. They do the actions. ↄTB

7

My collection

Write the words and expressions in your language in the 'My language' column of the Word list at the end of the book.

live	collect	soft toy	poster	stamp	leaf/leaves
30 thirty	**40** forty	**50** fifty	**60** sixty	**70** seventy	**80** eighty	**90** ninety	**100** one hundred

1 Listen, say and play. 🎧 1/8

2 Listen and read. 🎧 1/9

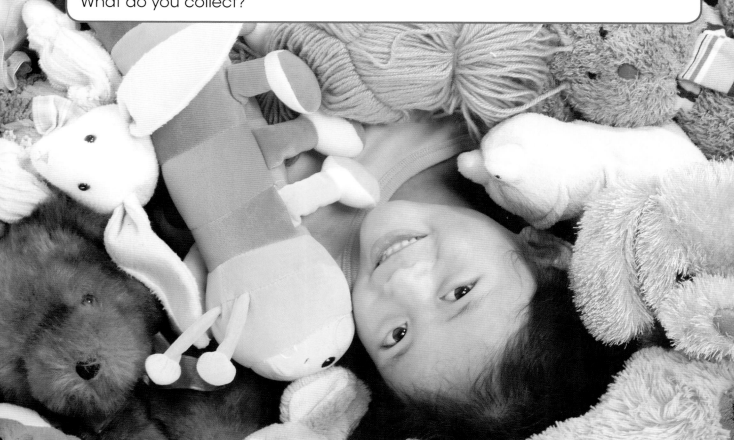

This is Sara-Lou. She lives in America. She collects soft toys. She has got fifty soft toys: teddy bears, dolls and toy animals.

Sara-Lou has got three brothers, Marcus, Jerry and Jonathon. They have got collections, too. Marcus collects posters. He has got thirty posters. Jerry has got eighty stamps and Jonathon collects leaves. He has got forty leaves.

What do you collect?

1 Pupils learn the new words and play *Hunt the Thimble*. ⊃TB
2 Pupils listen to the recording, follow the text and read it aloud.

3 Write and say.

| Name: _____ |
| Collects: _____ |
| How many: _____ |

| Name: _____ |
| Collects: _____ |
| How many: _____ |

| Name: _____ |
| Collects: _____ |
| How many: _____ |

| Name: _____ |
| Collects: _____ |
| How many: _____ |

Sara-Lou collects soft toys.
She's got fifty soft toys.

4 Listen and chant. 1/10

5 Look and talk.

What do you collect?

I collect dolls.

How many dolls have you got?

I've got thirty dolls.

3 Pupils complete the missing information about Sara-Lou and her brothers and talk about each collection.
4 Pupils listen to the chant and chant all together.
5 Pupils act out short dialogues. ☞TB

9

I like baking.

Write the words and expressions in your language in the 'My language' column of the Word list at the end of the book.

baking	cookie	gardening
hiking	travelling	Me too!

1 Listen, say and play. 1/11

2 Listen and read. 1/12

Grandma: What are you doing, Jeff?
Jeff: I'm baking cookies. I like baking and I love cookies!

Lucy: Hello, Betty! What are you doing?
Betty: I'm watering the tomatoes. I love gardening and I love tomatoes! Come and help me. We can make a tomato sandwich for lunch.

Mummy: Do you like hiking, Lizzie?
Lizzie: Yes, I do. Hiking is cool!
Daddy: I like hiking and I love travelling.
Lizzie: Me too!

1 Pupils learn the new words and play *Chinese Whispers.* ⊃TB
2 Pupils listen to the dialogues and read them aloud.

3 Write and read.

Jeff
Lizzie
Daddy
Betty

1 _____ likes tomatoes.

2 _____ likes baking.

3 _____ likes hiking.

4 _____ likes travelling.

4 Listen, number and chant.

5 Read and write.

Yes, I do.   No, I don't.

1 Do you like baking? _____

2 Do you like hiking? _____

3 Do you like gardening? _____

4 Do you like travelling? _____

3 Pupils complete the sentences with the correct names and read them aloud.
4 Pupils listen to the chant, number the pictures accordingly and chant all together.
5 Pupils write their own answers, then read the questions and answers aloud.

Wonderful world

What are your hobbies?

Archery is a great hobby. You need a bow and arrows and good eyesight to do it.

At the weekend I go to pottery classes. All you need is clay and your hands.

1 Circle and read.

archerybirdwatchingfishingpottery

2 Match and say.

clay

arrows

hands

good eyesight

Archery

Bird watching

fishing rod

bow

Fishing

Pottery

binoculars

camera

bird book

1 Pupils circle the names of hobbies and read them aloud.
2 Pupils match the words to the correct hobby and read them aloud.

I've got a new hobby. It's fishing. You need a fishing rod to do it. I like fishing with Daddy.

My favourite hobby is bird watching. You need a pair of binoculars, a bird book and a camera to take photos of the birds.

Class Project

Guess my hobby

Make a poster on an A3 sheet of paper describing your hobby. Then talk about your hobbies in pairs, asking questions and trying to guess what it is.

Is it ice skating?

Is it a sport?

Do you collect anything?

Can you do this sport in summer?

DVD Club

favourite

rose bush

postcard

lucky

magazine

1 Watch, tick and say.

 ☐

 ☐

 ☐

 ☐

 ☐

 ☐

2 Watch, write and match.

1 collect   a r _ _ e b _ sh

2 ride   st _ r _ es

3 write   p _ stc _ r _ s

4 plant   a h _ r _ e

3 Watch and say.

1 Pupils watch the DVD, tick the objects they see and say the words.
2 Pupils watch the DVD again, complete the words with the missing letters, then match them to the correct verbs.
3 Pupils watch the slideshows and repeat the words.

15

Review 1

1 Write and read.

> stories   karate   piano   photos   horse

1 Fred has got a camera. He takes ———— .

2 Kate likes sport. She does ———— .

3 Snap likes music. He plays the ———— .

4 Honey likes books. He writes ———— .

5 Chatty likes animals. She rides her ———— .

2 Listen, stick and read.

1 I have got 30 .

2 My daddy collects .

3 My mummy likes .

4 I often ride my .

5 I play .

6 He often writes .

3 Look and say.

I like gardening.

I don't like gardening.

1 Pupils complete the sentences with words from the box and read them aloud.
2 Pupils listen to the recording, stick the correct stickers and read the sentences aloud.
3 Pupils look at the picture and word cards from Unit 1 and say the sentences.

 **My hobby**

I can! 😊 😐 ☹

1 I understand sentences that I hear and I can write the numbers correctly. 🎧 1/15

2 I can describe a picture using full sentences.

3 I can read and understand sentences.

Sometimes, I write stories. ☐

She collects soft toys. ☐

Do you like baking? ☐

4 I can write sentences.

1 horse   my   every   I   day.   ride

_____ ☐

2 hiking.   like   I   gardening   and

_____ ☐

Unit 2 Wild animals

The giraffes are drinking our tea!

You will learn:
* the names of some wild animals
* to describe the appearance and habits of some animals
* to talk about animal records.

1 Listen and say. 🎧1/16

2 Play.

Alphabet corner

3 Listen and sing. 🎧1/17

At the zoo.

Write the words and expressions in your language in the 'My language' column of the Word list at the end of the book.

lion	dangerous	giraffe	gentle	tall
neck	zebra	stripe	Let's go home.	miss

1 Listen, say and play. ⊙1/18

2 Listen, read and make. ⊙1/19

Story corner

1 The lion's got a big mouth and big teeth!

Lions are dangerous.

2 Giraffes are gentle. They don't eat meat. They eat leaves from trees.

They are tall.

3 There are some black and white horses.

They're not horses. They're zebras. They have got black and white stripes.

4 There's Snap!

It's a wild crocodile. Be careful!

Let's go home. I miss Snap.

1 Pupils learn the new words and play *What's missing?* ⊃TB
2 Pupils listen to the dialogue, follow the story and read the sentences. ⊃TB

3 Read and circle.

1 Lions are dangerous.   T / F

2 Lions have got long necks.   T / F

3 Giraffes are black and white.   T / F

4 Giraffes eat leaves from trees.   T / F

5 Zebras have got stripes.   T / F

6 Zebras eat meat.   T / F

4 Make, listen and sing.

5 Match, write and read.

1

**lion   dangerous
a big mouth and big teeth
meat**

2

**giraffe   tall
a long neck and long legs
leaves**

3

**zebra   gentle
black and white stripes
grass**

It's a _____ . It's _____ .

It's got _____ .

It eats _____ .

3 Pupils read the sentences and circle T (*true*) or F (*false*).
4 Pupils make animal masks, listen to the song and sing all together acting out the animal roles in groups. ƏTB
5 Pupils match the photos with the correct boxes. They choose one animal, complete the description
  using the phrases in the box and read it aloud.

21

A red fox

Write the words and expressions in your language in the 'My language' column of the Word list at the end of the book.

| fox | forest | beautiful | hunt |
| mouse/mice | insect | egg | difficult | see |

1 Listen, say and play. 1/21

2 Listen and read. 1/22

This is a red fox. It is a wild animal. It lives in a forest. It has got red and white fur and a beautiful tail. It can jump and swim very well. It hunts small animals such as mice and birds. It eats fruit, insects and eggs, too. It's difficult to see a red fox in a forest but you can see a red fox at the zoo.

1 Pupils learn the new words and play the *Guessing Game*. ⊃TB
2 Pupils listen to the recording, follow the text and read it aloud.

3 Read, circle and listen.

1 Does the red fox live in a forest?

   a Yes, it does.   **b** No, it doesn't.

2 Does the red fox hunt horses?

   a Yes, it does.   **b** No, it doesn't.

3 Can the red fox swim?

   a Yes, it can.   **b** No, it can't.

4 Does the red fox eat fruit?

   a Yes, it does.   **b** No, it doesn't.

5 Does the red fox eat cheese?

   a Yes, it does.   **b** No, it doesn't.

4 Listen and sing.

5 Write and read.

mice   fox   fruit   lives   wild

This is a red _____ .

It is a _____ animal.

It _____ in a forest.

It hunts _____ and birds.

It eats _____ , insects

and eggs, too.

3 Pupils read the questions, circle the correct answers and listen to check.
4 Pupils listen to the song and sing all together.
5 Pupils complete the text using the words from the box and read the sentences aloud.

23

Lesson 3

Biggest and smallest

Write the words and expressions in your language in the 'My language' column of the Word list at the end of the book.

> I think…   biggest   land animal   elephant   cheetah   bird
> ostrich   question   smallest   I don't know.   hummingbird

1 Listen, say and play. 🎧 1/25

2 Listen and read. 🎧 1/26

Boy: Let's do a quiz about wild animals.
Girl: Oh, yes. I love animals.
Boy: What is the tallest animal?
Girl: I think it's a giraffe.
Boy: Yes, it is. It's very tall and it eats leaves from the trees.

Boy: What's the biggest land animal?
Girl: An elephant?
Boy: Yes! It's really big.

Girl: I've got a question: What's the smallest bird?
Boy: I don't know.
Girl: It's a hummingbird. It's very small.

Boy: What's the fastest animal?
Girl: A cheetah?
Boy: Yes! A cheetah can run very fast.

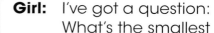

Boy: What's the biggest bird?
Girl: I know! It's an ostrich.
Boy: Yes, it is!

1 Pupils learn the new words and play *Find Your Pair.* ⊃TB
2 Pupils listen to the dialogue and read it aloud.

3 Read and stick.

1 An

is the biggest land animal.

2 A

is the smallest bird.

3 A

is the fastest animal.

4 A

is the tallest animal.

4 Listen and chant. 🎵 1/27

5 Write and read.

1 animal.   the tallest   is   A giraffe

_____

2 the biggest   An elephant   land animal.   is

_____

3 A cheetah   the fastest   is   animal.

_____

4 is   the smallest   A hummingbird   bird.

_____

3 Pupils read the sentences aloud and stick the correct stickers.
4 Pupils listen to the chant and chant all together. ⊃TB
5 Pupils write the sentences and read them aloud.

25

Wonderful world

> Dolphins live in the water, but they are not fish. They are nice to people and love playing. They hunt small fish. They are very clever.

1 Circle and read.

1 dangerous   clever   snow   nice
2 bear   fish   tree   bird
3 tail   run   swim   jump
4 hunt   fly   eat   skin
5 tongue   fur   skin   change

> Chameleons live on trees. They have got very long tails and tongues. Their skin can change colour.

2 Look and write.

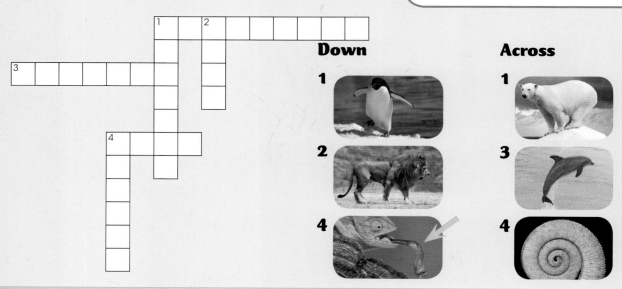

Down

1
2
4

Across

1
3
4

1 Pupils circle the odd words out and read them aloud.
2 Pupils look at the clues and complete the crossword puzzle.

Penguins are birds, but they can't fly. They like swimming and can jump well. Penguins can eat snow!

Polar bears are the biggest bears. They are very dangerous animals. Polar bears can swim well and run fast. Their fur is white, but their skin is black!

Class Project

Class zoo

Choose one animal and make an arts & crafts project. Then talk about this animal in a few sentences.

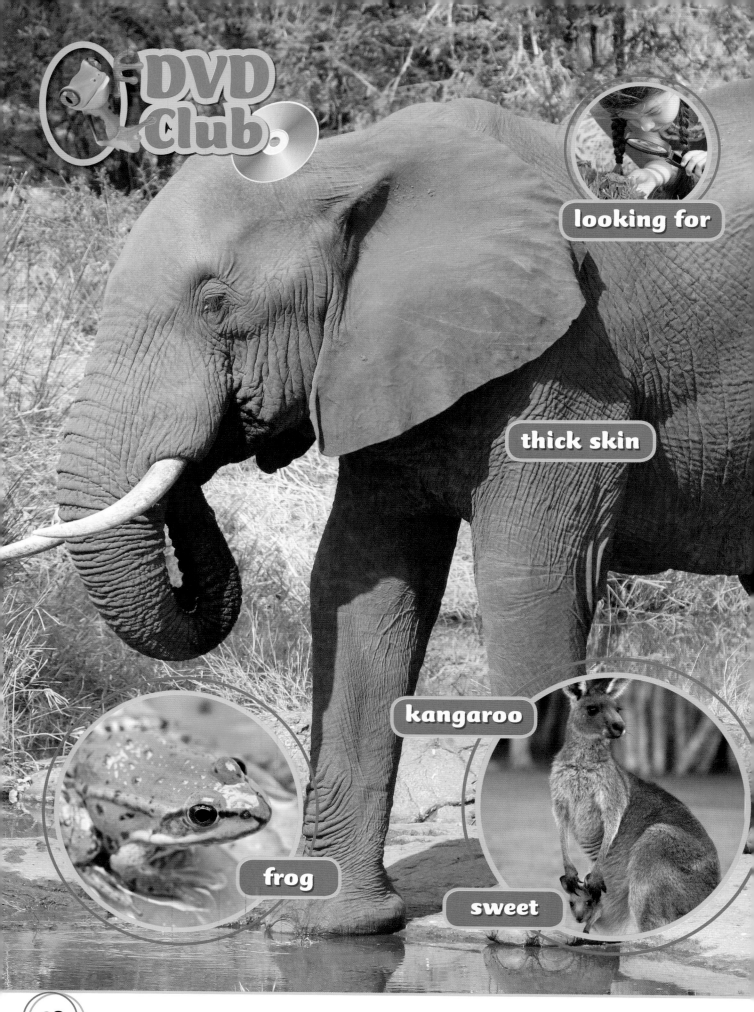

DVD Club

looking for

thick skin

kangaroo

frog

sweet

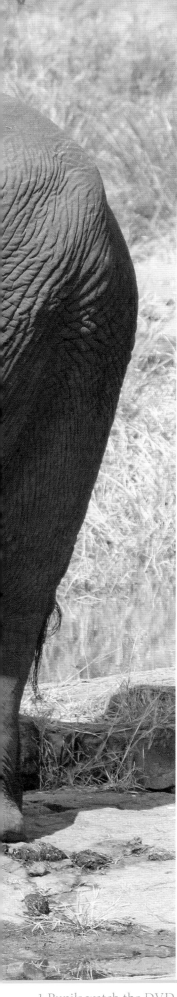

1 Watch, write and read.

1 Sam thinks his cat, Tiggie, is *b*_____ .
2 Tiggie is brown with black *s*_____ .
3 Becky says the cat looks very *g*_____ .
4 Becky thinks the baby kangaroo is very
  *s*_____ .

2 Watch, circle and read.

1 Becky's favourite animal lives in Australia /
  Africa and Asia .
2 It has got fur / thick skin .
3 It is big / small .
4 It's an elephant / a kangaroo .

5 Sam's favourite animal is a cat, but he likes
  another animal too. It is a bird / land animal .
6 It lives in Africa / Australia .
7 It likes to run / jump .
8 It's an elephant / a kangaroo .

3 Watch and say.

1 Pupils watch the DVD, complete the sentences and read the sentences aloud.
2 Pupils watch the DVD again, circle the correct answers and read the sentences aloud.
3 Pupils watch the slideshows and repeat the words.

29

Review 2

1 Read and write.

> hamster   duck   lion   lamb   cheetah   goldfish   cow
> dog   cat   giraffe   horse   pig   crocodile   sheep   canary
> hummingbird   elephant   fox   parrot   ostrich   rabbit

Pets	Farm animals	Wild animals
☐	☐	☐
☐	☐	☐
☐	☐	☐
☐	☐	☐
☐	☐	☐
☐	☐	☐
☐		☐
		☐

2 Listen and tick. 1/28

3 Write and read.

These are _____ (zebras/horses).

They're _____ (wild/farm) animals. They

_____ (live/hunt) in Africa. They eat

_____ (meat/grass). They have got black

and _____ (white/brown) stripes. They are

_____ (beautiful/dangerous) animals.

1 Pupils write the names of the animals in the table.
2 Pupils listen to the recording and use the table to tick the names of the animals they hear.
3 Pupils complete the text about zebras and read it aloud.

 **Wild animals**

I can! 😊 😐 ☹️

1 I understand sentences that I hear and I can write the numbers correctly. 🎧 1/29

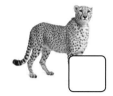 ☐ ☐  ☐  ☐ ☐

2 I can describe a picture using full sentences.

3 I can read and understand sentences.

Does a red fox live in a forest? ☐

Giraffes have got long necks. ☐

The hummingbird is the smallest bird. ☐

4 I can write sentences.

1 the fastest   A cheetah   animal.   is

_____ ☐

2 Do   live   Africa?   in   lions

_____ ☐

Unit 3 Jobs

It's a street market.
We can buy food here.

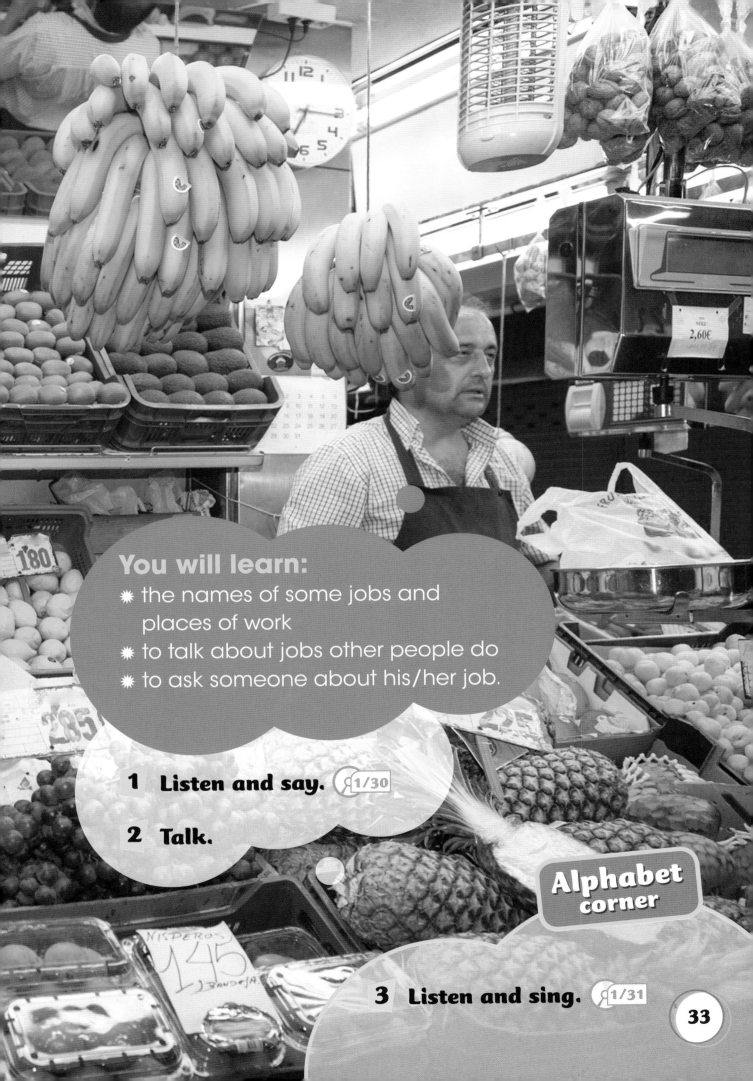

You will learn:
* the names of some jobs and places of work
* to talk about jobs other people do
* to ask someone about his/her job.

1 Listen and say. 1/30

2 Talk.

Alphabet corner

3 Listen and sing. 1/31

33

Where is Snap?

Write the words and expressions in your language in the 'My language' column of the Word list at the end of the book.

> doctor nurse work hospital
> Here you are. restaurant chef waiter hungry

1 Listen, say and play.

2 Listen, read and make.

Story corner

1 Pupils learn the new words and play *Find your pair*. ⊙TB
2 Pupils listen to the dialogue, follow the story and read the sentences. ⊙TB

3 **Write and say.**

teacher   nurse   doctor   chef   waiter   children

Hospital

School

Restaurant

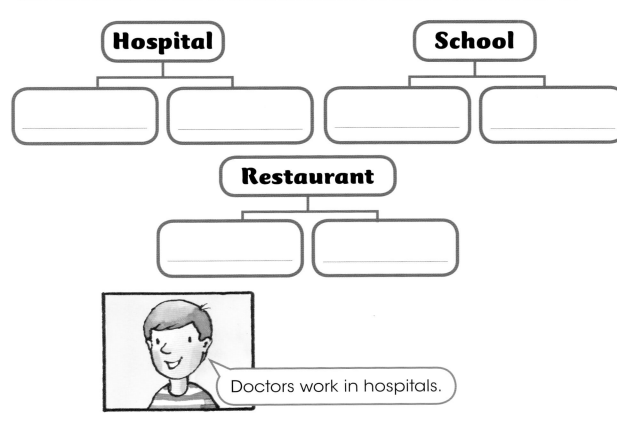

Doctors work in hospitals.

4 **Listen and chant.** 1/34

5 **Write and read.**

1   in   a school.   works   A teacher

_____

2   wears   a uniform.   A waiter

_____

3   A nurse   the doctor.   helps

_____

4   a restaurant.   in   works   A chef

_____

3 Pupils complete the diagrams and say who works where.
4 Pupils listen to the chant and chant all together.
5 Pupils write the sentences and read them aloud.

35

He's a vet.

Write the words and expressions in your language in the 'My language' column of the Word list at the end of the book.

vet	treat	kitten	touch
need		medicine	

1 Listen, say and play. 1/35

2 Listen and read. 1/36

This is John Walker. He is a vet. He works in an animal hospital. He treats pets and farm animals: cats, dogs, horses and lambs. He doesn't treat wild animals.

Today, John is treating a kitten. John looks at its eyes, ears and teeth. He touches the kitten's tummy, too. The kitten is ill. It needs some medicine.

John is a good vet. He likes animals and he likes his job.

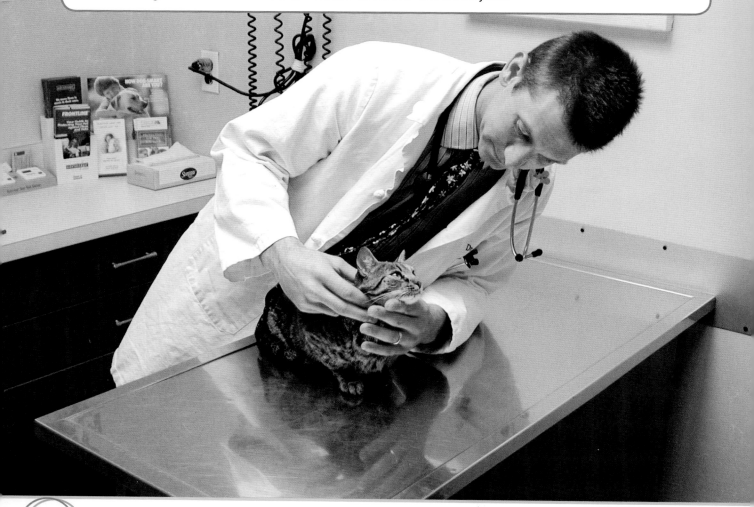

1 Pupils learn the new words and play *Dominoes*. ⊕TB
2 Pupils listen to the recording, follow the text and read it aloud.

3 Read and circle.

1 John Walker works in:
   a a school.
   b a restaurant.
   c an animal hospital.

3 Today, he is treating:
   a a rabbit.
   b a kitten.
   c a dog.

5 The kitten is:
   a OK.
   b ill.
   c happy.

2 He doesn't treat:
   a dogs.
   b horses.
   c foxes.

4 He touches the kitten's:
   a eyes.
   b teeth.
   c tummy.

6 John Walker is a good:
   a vet.
   b doctor.
   c teacher.

4 Listen and chant. 1/37

5 Number, listen and talk. 1/38

What can we do?

Hello!

Good boy, Spot.

This is my dog, Spot. He's sad. Is he ill?

Thank you. Goodbye.

Goodbye.

Let me touch his tummy and look at his ears.

Yes, he's ill.

Hello. What's the problem?

Spot needs some medicine. Here you are.

---

3 Pupils circle the correct answers and read the sentences aloud.
4 Pupils listen to the chant and chant all together.
5 Pupils number the speech bubbles, listen to the recording to check their answers and act out the dialogue. ⊃TB

My mum is a firefighter.

Write the words and expressions in your language in the 'My language' column of the Word list at the end of the book.

firefighter	drive	fire engine	important	postman
letter	parcel	pilot	fly	exciting

1 Listen, say and play. 1/39

2 Listen and read. 1/40

George: Look at these photos of my family. This is my mummy.
Emily: Wow! Is your mummy a firefighter?
George: Yes, she is. She drives a fire engine! It's a dangerous job, but it's very important. Firefighters help people.

Emily: Is this your daddy?
George: Yes, it is.
Emily: What's his job?
George: He's a postman. He delivers letters and parcels.

Emily: Who's that?
George: That's my Aunt Lucy. She's my mummy's sister. She's a pilot. She flies planes. It's a very exciting job!
Emily: You've got a great family!

1 Pupils learn the new words and play the *Echo Game*. ⊙TB
2 Pupils listen to the dialogue and read it aloud.

3 Stick and read.

1 George's mummy is a ⬭ .

2 She drives a ⬭ .

3 George's daddy delivers ⬭ and ⬭ .

4 Aunt Lucy is a ⬭ .

5 She ⬭ planes.

4 Listen and sing. 🎵 1/41

5 Write and read.

(flies   drives   delivers)

(letters   a fire engine   parcels   planes)

1 Mummy _____ .

2 Daddy _____

  and _____ .

3 Aunt Lucy _____ .

6 Play.

3 Pupils stick the stickers in the correct place and read the sentences aloud.
4 Pupils listen to the song and sing all together.
5 Pupils write sentences using the words from the boxes and read them aloud.
6 Pupils play *Chinese Whispers*.

39

Wonderful world

Julie is an artist. She loves drawing and painting pictures. She draws and paints people, animals and nature.

1 Look and circle.

m	u	s	i	c	i	a	n	u	t	h	e	a	t	r	e
b	d	s	o	n	g	f	i	g	g	a	c	t	o	r	j
p	a	i	n	t	i	n	g	a	p	n	a	t	u	r	e
a	r	t	i	s	t	h	c	k	c	o	n	c	e	r	t

artist   painting
nature   musician
song   concert
actor   theatre

2 Write and read.

1 Bob, the musician, _p_____ the guitar, _s_____

songs and gives _c_____ .

2 Julie, the artist, _d_____ and _p_____ pictures.

3 De Dong, the actor, _w_____ in a theatre and wears

_b_____ clothes.

1 Pupils find and circle the hidden words.
2 Pupils complete the sentences with the correct words.

Bob is a musician. He can play the guitar and the trumpet.
He writes and sings songs. He often gives concerts.

De Dong and Ai Fang are actors. They work in a theatre.
They can dance and sing. They often wear beautiful clothes.

Class Project

Jobs

In pairs, make a poster about a person and their job. Highlight the typical features of this job and talk about it.

DVD Club

brave firefighters

tired

look after

operation

cleaning

1 Watch and tick.

	doctor	firefighter	musician	vet
Becky's dad				
Becky's mum				
Sam's mum				
Sam's dad				

2 Watch and match.

dog   mouth

ears   nurses

girl   operation

medicine   teeth

3 Watch and say.

1 Pupils watch the DVD and tick which person does which job.
2 Pupils watch the DVD again and match the words to Becky's mum or Becky's dad.
3 Pupils watch the slideshows and repeat the words.

43

Review 3

1 **Write and read.**

> a pilot   a firefighter   a nurse   a vet

> treats animals that are ill   flies planes
> drives a fire engine   helps the doctor

1 _____ .

2 _____ .

3 _____ .

4 _____ .

2 **Listen and number.** 1/42

3 **Play.**

1 Pupils write the sentences and read them aloud.
2 Pupils listen to the recording and number the photos accordingly.
3 Pupils play *Guess the Identity*. ⊙TB

 **Jobs**

I can!

1 I understand sentences that I hear and I can write the numbers correctly. 1/43

2 I can describe a picture using full sentences.

3 I can read and understand sentences.

The rabbit needs medicine. ☐

My aunt's job is very dangerous. ☐

The vet is treating the dog. ☐

4 I can write sentences.

1   doesn't   in   He   the hospital.   work

_____ ☐

2   don't   Vets   people.   treat

_____ ☐

I love pizza.

You will learn:
* to order in a restaurant
* the names of some food
* to describe and prepare some dishes.

1 Listen and say. 2/1

2 Make and say.

Alphabet corner

3 Listen and sing. 2/2

Can I have some chicken, please?

Write the words and expressions in your language in the 'My language' column of the Word list at the end of the book.

fish and chips	vegetable	menu	tomato soup	chicken
chocolate cake		one more		Enjoy your meal.
delicious		glass of milk		Help yourself.

1 Listen, say and play. 2/3

Story corner

2 Listen, read and make. 2/4

1 What are you eating?

I've got some fish and chips, some vegetables and a pizza.

2 Can I have an egg sandwich and some cheese, please?

3 Here you are. A glass of milk and some chocolate cake for you.

Thank you.

4 My chicken is delicious. Help yourself, Snap.

Poor Snap!

Oh no, my tummy, my tummy.

1 Pupils learn the new words and play *Sentence String*. ⊙TB
2 Pupils listen to the dialogue, follow the story and read the sentences. ⊙TB

3 Match and say.

some fish and chips
some vegetables
a pizza
some chicken
some chocolate cake
some tomato soup
an egg sandwich
some cheese
some milk

Can I have some fish and chips, some vegetables and a pizza, please?

4 Listen and sing. 2/5

5 Write and read.

Can I have an egg sandwich, please?

Here you are.

cheese   chicken   fish and chips   tomato soup   milk

1 Can I have some _____ , please?

2 Can I have some _____ , please?

3 Can I have some _____ , please?

4 Can I have a glass of _____ , please?

5 Can I have some _____ , please?

3 Pupils match the food the characters order and repeat the order.
4 Pupils listen to the song and sing all together. ⊃TB
5 Pupils complete the sentences and read the sentences aloud in pairs.

49

Pumpkin Farm

Write the words and expressions in your language in the 'My language' column of the Word list at the end of the book.

farmer	grow	carrot	lettuce
potato	pumpkin	village	shop assistant

1 Listen, say and play. 2/6

2 Listen and read. 2/7

> This is Jessica. She lives on a farm with her family. Her daddy works on the farm. He is a farmer. He grows carrots, lettuces, potatoes and pumpkins. Her mummy sells the vegetables in a shop in the village. She is a shop assistant.
>
> Jessica has got a brother, John, and a baby sister. Jessica and John help their parents on the farm and in the shop.

1 Pupils learn and say the new words and play *Chinese Whispers*. ⊙TB
2 Pupils listen to the recording, follow the text and read it aloud.

3 Read and circle.

1 Jessica's daddy:
   a sells vegetables in the shop.
   b grows vegetables.
   c drives a truck.

2 Jessica's daddy grows:
   a potatoes.
   b apples.
   c tomatoes.

3 Jessica's mummy is:
   a a farmer.
   b a shop assistant.
   c a teacher.

4 Jessica has got:
   a one brother and two sisters.
   b one sister.
   c one brother and one sister.

5 Jessica's brother's name is:
   a John.
   b Josh.
   c Jake.

6 Jessica:
   a rides a bike.
   b helps in the shop.
   c plays in the garden.

4 Play.

5 Read and draw.

In my garden I grow vegetables: pumpkins, tomatoes and lettuces.
There are two apple trees and three pear trees.

3 Pupils read the text again, then they read the sentences and choose the correct answer.
4 Pupils play *Sentence String*. ⊙TB
5 Pupils read the text and draw a picture.

51

Gingerbread cookies

Write the words and expressions in your language in the 'My language' column of the Word list at the end of the book.

cup	flour	sugar	butter	ginger
teaspoon	put	bowl	add	mix	bake

1 Listen, say and play. 2/8

2 Listen and read. 2/9

Brenda: Let's make gingerbread cookies!
Gina: Good idea! What do we need?
Brenda: We need one cup of flour, one cup of sugar, some butter, two eggs and one teaspoon of ginger.

Brenda: Let's put the flour and ginger into a bowl.
Gina: OK.
Brenda: Now add the butter, sugar and eggs and mix it all together.
Gina: Ready!

Brenda: We need to bake the cookies for ten minutes. Mummy, can you help us, please?

1 Pupils learn the new words and play *What's missing?* ⊃TB
2 Pupils listen to the dialogue and read it aloud.

3 **Stick and read.**

Gingerbread cookies

✓ one cup of _____

✓ _____ of sugar

✓ some _____

✓ two _____

✓ one _____ of ginger

4 **Number and read.**

☐ Add the butter, sugar and eggs.

☐ Put the flour and ginger into a bowl.

☐ Bake the cookies for ten minutes.

☐ Mix it all together.

yummy!

5 **Listen and chant.** 2/10

3 Pupils stick the stickers in the correct place.
4 Pupils number the recipe instructions and read the recipe aloud.
5 Pupils listen to the chant and chant all together.

Wonderful world

Children in Italy love spaghetti bolognese. To cook it, you need some tomatoes, onions, meat and pasta. It's delicious!

In America, children like making pumpkin pies. To bake a pumpkin pie, you need some eggs, sugar, salt, milk, flour, ginger and pumpkin. It's easy to make and yummy!

1 Match and read.

salt

pasta

yeast

sugar

2 Look and write.

1 e a m l _____

2 a s l t _____

3 m m y u y _____

4 s g u r a _____

5 t i t e h g a p s _____

6 i e p _____

1 Pupils match the words with the photos and read the words aloud.
2 Pupils unscramble the words and write them on the lines.

In England, children often have fish and chips. You fry some fish and potatoes for 10 to 15 minutes. It's a great meal!

Naan bread is very popular in India. You mix water, butter, flour and yeast and bake it. It's delicious and very easy to make.

Class Project

Strawberry desserts

Make a strawberry dessert using plasticine. Then write down a real recipe for a dessert made of strawberries. Exchange your recipes with other groups.

Pupils do a class project.

DVD Club

cup of tea

salad

ice cream

plate

greenhouse

1 Watch and match.

box

picking

2 Watch, circle and read.

1 Becky and Sam   are / aren't   very hungry.

2 Becky's dad calls the   chef / waiter .

3 Becky   likes / doesn't like   her pizza.

4 Sam   likes / doesn't like   salad with fish and chips.

5 The man in the film is   eating / picking   tomatoes.

3 Watch and say.

1 Pupils watch the DVD and match the food items with the characters.
2 Pupils watch the DVD again, circle the correct answers and read the sentences aloud.
3 Pupils watch the slideshows and repeat the words.

Review 4

1 Listen, stick and read. 2/11

1 My favourite food is

.

2 My favourite food is

.

3 My favourite food is

.

4 My favourite food is

.

5 My favourite food is

.

6 My favourite food is

.

2 Write and read.

1 the menu. Here is

_____

2 I have Can please? vegetables some

_____

3 you? for And

_____

4 Can soup have I tomato , please? some

_____

3 Talk.

1 Pupils listen to the recording, stick the correct stickers and read the sentences aloud.
2 Pupils write the words into the correct order and read the sentences.
3 Pupils act out the dialogue between a waiter and a customer. ⊃TB

 **Food**

I can!

I can! 😊 😐 ☹️

1 I understand sentences that I hear and I can write the numbers correctly. (2/12)

 ☐  ☐  ☐  ☐  ☐ 😊

2 I can describe a picture using full sentences.

 😊

3 I can read and understand sentences.

Can I have some soup, please? ☐ He sells vegetables in a small shop. ☐ Bake the cakes for ten minutes. ☐ 😊

4 I can write sentences.

1 a village. live in They ☐

2 yourself cookie. to Help a ☐ 😊

Pupils do the self-evaluation.

59

My week

At the weekend, I usually go roller skating.

You will learn:
* the names of the days of the week
* to talk about your timetable
* to talk about morning and evening routines.

1 Listen and say. 2/13

2 Talk.

3 Listen and sing. 2/14

Fred's timetable

Write the words and expressions in your language in the 'My language' column of the Word list at the end of the book.

timetable	difficult	Monday	Tuesday
Wednesday	Thursday	Friday	busy
	later	easy	I'm sorry.

1 Listen, say and play. 2/15

Story corner

2 Listen, read and make. 2/16

1 Pupils learn and say the new words and play *Find Your Pair*. ⊃TB
2 Pupils listen to the dialogue, follow the story and read the sentences. ⊃TB

3 Write and say.

On Mondays, I play football.

football   the piano   a bike   TV   swimming   the guitar
a book   karate   chess   a horse   tennis

_____
Monday

_____
Tuesday

_____
Wednesday

_____
Thursday

_____
Friday

4 Listen and chant. 2/17

5 Write and read.

1 On _____ , I _____ .

2 On _____ , I _____ .

3 On _____ , I _____ .

3 Pupils complete Fred's diary with the phrases from the box and say the sentences.
4 Pupils listen to the chant and chant all together.
5 Pupils write down what they do during the week and read the sentences aloud.

63

At the weekend

Write the words and expressions in your language in the 'My language' column of the Word list at the end of the book.

Saturday	Sunday	week	brush	paint
together	musician	violin	flute	give a concert

1 **Listen, say and play.** 2/18

2 **Listen and read.** 2/19

Alice likes weekends. Saturday and Sunday are her favourite days of the week. She plays and has fun. Today is Saturday. Alice and her three brothers have got brushes and they are painting together.

Alice's parents are musicians. On Sundays the family plays music together. Alice plays the piano. John and Cody play violins and Tom plays the guitar. Their mummy plays the flute and their daddy plays the trumpet. Sometimes they give concerts.

1 Pupils learn and say the new words, then play *Missing Letters*. ⏎TB
2 Pupils listen to the recording, follow the text and read it aloud.

3 Read and circle.

1. Alice likes Saturdays and Sundays. T / F
2. Today is Sunday. T / F
3. Alice's mummy is a musician. T / F
4. Alice plays the violin. T / F
5. John plays the violin. T / F
6. The family sometimes gives concerts. T / F

4 Listen, sing and draw.

5 Write, listen and read. 2/21

> meet   homework   Sunday   music   books   bike

My favourite day is _____ . I can play and have fun

on Sundays. I _____ my friends, go to the cinema or

ride my _____ . I also read _____ and

listen to _____ . I don't do my _____ on

Sundays. I do it on Fridays.

3 Pupils read the sentences and circle T (*true*) or F (*false*).
4 Pupils listen to the song and sing all together. They draw a picture of their favourite weekend activity.
5 Pupils complete the text with words from the box, listen to the recording to check their answers and read the text aloud.

65

In the morning

Write the words and expressions in your language in the 'My language' column of the Word list at the end of the book.

> bored   morning   wake up   early
> get washed   get dressed   have breakfast
> brush our teeth   have dinner   evening
> I'd like to sleep late.   I'd like to stay up late.

1 Listen, say and play. 2/22

2 Listen and read. 2/23

1

Ben: Oh, Monica, I am so bored. Every morning we wake up early, get washed, get dressed, have breakfast, brush our teeth and go to school.

 2

Monica: It's the same every evening. We have dinner, do our homework, play computer games, get washed, brush our teeth and go to bed early. What would you like to do, Ben?

3

Ben: I'd like to sleep late every day, have breakfast in bed and watch TV with Dad. Then I'd like to go to the cinema. In the evening, I'd like to play computer games and stay up late.

Monica: I know, I know. You'd like every day to be Saturday!

1 Pupils learn and say the new words and play the *Guessing Game.* ⏵TB
2 Pupils listen to the dialogue and read it aloud.

3 Stick and read.

Every morning Ben and Monica …	Every evening Ben and Monica …	Ben would like to …
get washed	do their homework	sleep late
get dressed	play computer games	go to the cinema
go to school	brush their teeth	watch TV with Dad

4 Listen and sing. 2/24

5 Write and read.

1 In the morning I _____ ,

but I'd like to _____ .

2 In the evening I _____ ,

but I'd like to _____ .

3 Pupils stick the stickers in the correct places and read the sentences aloud.
4 Pupils listen to the song and sing all together. They mime the actions. ⊃TB
5 Pupils write sentences about themselves and read them aloud.

67

Wonderful world

In the evening I water the flowers in the garden. It is fun!

In my family, we all help at home. I usually clean my room.

1 Write and read.

home?   help   at   How   you   do

_____

2 Read and circle.

1 **a** water the flowers
   b clean your room
   c get dressed

2 **a** water the flowers
   b clean your room
   c do the washing up

3 **a** brush your teeth
   b water the flowers
   c do the washing up

4 **a** clean your room
   b set the table
   c do your homework

1 Pupils put the words in the correct order and read the question aloud.
2 Pupils circle the correct expressions.

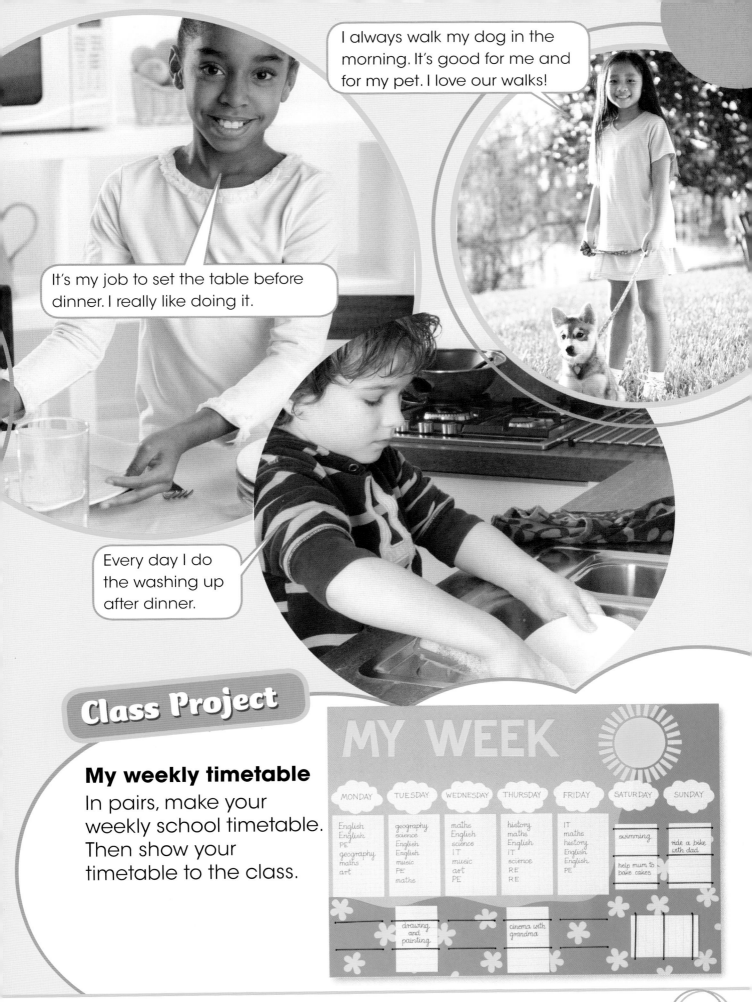

I always walk my dog in the morning. It's good for me and for my pet. I love our walks!

It's my job to set the table before dinner. I really like doing it.

Every day I do the washing up after dinner.

Class Project

My weekly timetable

In pairs, make your weekly school timetable. Then show your timetable to the class.

MY WEEK

MONDAY	TUESDAY	WEDNESDAY	THURSDAY	FRIDAY	SATURDAY	SUNDAY
English English PE geography maths art	geography science English English music PE maths	maths English science IT music art PE	history maths English IT science RE RE	IT maths history English English PE	swimming	ride a bike with dad
					help mum to bake cakes	
	drawing and painting		cinema with grandma			

DVD Club

rock

climbing

art club

ropes

fit

1 Watch and write.

do homework
go swimming
paint pictures
play football
watch TV
write stories

Monday _____

Tuesday _____

Wednesday _____

Thursday _____

Friday _____

2 Watch, circle and read.

1  likes Saturdays best.

2   likes Sundays best.

3  wants to do something exciting this weekend.

4  cousin is Anna.

5 thinks climbing looks dangerous.

3 Watch and say.

1 Pupils watch the DVD and write down what Sam does each day.
2 Pupils watch the DVD again, circle the correct photo and read the sentences aloud.
3 Pupils watch the slideshows and repeat the words.

Review 5

1 Write and read.

1   I wake _____ early in the morning.

2   I get _____ in the morning.

3   I _____ my teeth in the morning and in the evening.

4   I go to _____ early every day.

5   I play the _____ every Saturday.

2 Write and play.

M __ nd __ y   T __ esda __   Wedn __ s __ ay

T__ ur __ da __   F__ id __ y

S __ tu __ day   Su __ d __ y

3 Listen and circle. 2/25

My name is Jim. I like playing / listening to music and painting / drawing pictures. On Mondays / Wednesdays I have music lessons. One day I'd like to give a concert at school. On Saturdays / Sundays I paint pictures at home with my parents / friends . Today I am painting a garden / forest . I'd like to give this picture to my grandma / aunt for her birthday.

1 Pupils complete the sentences and read them aloud.
2 Pupils complete the days of the week and play *Chinese Whispers*. ⊃TB
3 Pupils listen to the recording and circle the correct words.

 **My week**

I can!

1 I understand sentences that I hear and I can write the numbers correctly. ⟨2/26⟩

2 I can describe a picture using full sentences.

3 I can read and understand sentences.

This is my timetable. ☐   There isn't time to do homework on Mondays. ☐   I'd like to sleep late in the morning. ☐

4 I can write sentences.

1   My   day   favourite   Sunday.   is
_____ ☐

2   you   Do   musical   any   play   instruments?
_____ ☐

Unit 6
My favourite season

I'm happy when it's cold.

74

You will learn:
* the names of the seasons
* to compare the weather in different seasons
* to talk about your travel plans.

1 Listen and say. 2/27

2 Play.

Alphabet corner

3 Listen and sing. 2/28

I like spring.

Write the words and expressions in your language in the 'My language' column of the Word list at the end of the book.

> spring   sunflower   seed   plant   wait   month   March
> April   May   June   July   August   next year

1 Listen, say and play. 2/29

Story corner

2 Listen, read and make. 2/30

1 Pupils learn and say the new words and play *Hunt the Thimble*. ⊕TB
2 Pupils listen to the dialogue, follow the story and read the sentences. ⊕TB

3 Write and read.

1 _____ and _____ like spring very much.

2 _____ has got a sunflower seed.

3 _____ is hungry.

4 _____ wants a beautiful big sunflower, too.

5 _____ says they can buy more seeds at the market.

4 Listen and match. 2/31

5 Write and read.

1 _____ , _____ and _____ are spring months.

2 _____ , _____ and _____ are summer months.

3 Pupils complete the sentences with the appropriate names and read them aloud.
4 Pupils listen to the recording and match the characters with the correct picture.
5 Pupils write down the missing months of the year and read the sentences aloud.

What's the weather like in autumn?

Write the words and expressions in your language in the 'My language' column of the Word list at the end of the book.

> autumn   September   warm   go for a walk   campfire
> toast   sausage   October   get ready   November

1 Listen, say and play. 2/32

2 Listen and read. 2/33

Autumn is my family's favourite season.

In September it's warm and we often go for a walk in the forest. The trees look beautiful because their leaves are red, yellow and brown. We take lots of photos. In this photo we're having a campfire. We're making some toast and cooking sausages. Yummy!

In October the leaves fall from the trees. The days get shorter. The wild animals get ready for winter. In November it gets colder and it often rains.

1 Pupils learn and say the new words, then play *Chinese Whispers*. ⟳TB
2 Pupils listen to the recording, follow the text and read it aloud.

3 Write and read.

1 September, _O_____ and November are the autumn months.

2 It's nice to go for a _w_____ in the forest.

3 The leaves are red, yellow and _b_____ in autumn.

4 You can make toast and cook _s_____ on a campfire.

5 In October, the days are _s_____ than in September.

6 In November it often _r_____ .

4 Read and circle.

1 In winter it's warmer / colder than in autumn.

2 In summer the flowers are bigger / smaller than in spring.

3 In autumn the days are longer / shorter than in summer.

4 In spring the wild animals are happier / sadder than in winter.

5 Listen, number and chant. 2/34

3 Pupils complete the sentences with the correct words and read them aloud.
4 Pupils circle the correct adjectives and read the sentences aloud.
5 Pupils listen to the chant, number the pictures accordingly and chant all together.

To the mountains

Write the words and expressions in your language in the 'My language' column of the Word list at the end of the book.

> go away   December   mountain   January   February
> learn   lower   highest   skier

1 Listen, say and play. 2/35

2 Listen and read. 2/36

✔ **Myra:**
Hi, Bartek! Are you going away for Christmas?

✔ **Bartek:**
No, I'm not going away in December. I'm going skiing in the Tatra mountains in January. And you?

✔ **Myra:**
I'm going to the Scottish mountains in February. I can't ski but I'd like to learn.

✔ **Bartek:**
Great! Can you swim?

✔ **Myra:**
Yes, I can.

✔ **Bartek:**
Well, skiing is easier than swimming. Are the Scottish mountains high?

✔ **Myra:**
Yes, they are, but they're lower than the Alps. What about the Tatra mountains?

✔ **Bartek:**
They're the highest mountains in Poland, but they're lower than the Alps, too.

✔ **Myra:**
Are you a good skier?

✔ **Bartek:**
Yes, I am, but my parents are faster.

✔ **Myra:**
I'm sure you're not slower than them!

1 Pupils learn and say the new words and play the *Seasons Game*. ⊃TB
2 Pupils listen to the dialogue and read it aloud.

3 **Circle and read.**

1 Bartek is going away in December / January .

2 Myra is going away in January / February .

3 Myra can / can't ski.

4 The Tatra mountains are higher / lower than the Alps.

5 Bartek skis faster / slower than his parents.

4 **Listen and stick.** 2/37

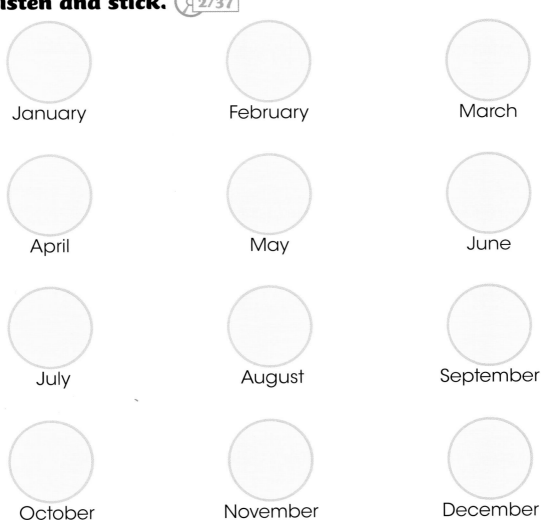

January

February

March

April

May

June

July

August

September

October

November

December

5 **Talk.**

I'm going away in _July._

I'm going away with _my parents._

I'd like to learn _to ride a horse._

3 Pupils circle the correct words and read the sentences aloud.
4 Pupils listen to the recording and stick the stickers in the correct places.
5 Pupils look at the table and talk in pairs about their plans. ᗒTB

81

Wonderful world

Summer in Australia is from December to February. Lots of people spend Christmas at the beach. It's really hot and there isn't any snow!

Autumn in Australia is in March, April and May. The weather is usually mild and the forests look beautiful. The mornings are sometimes foggy in the countryside.

1 Read and circle.

1 Australia is hot in January.   T / F
2 It often snows at Christmas in Australia.   T / F
3 Winter in Australia is colder than in Europe.   T / F
4 You can go skiing in Australia.   T / F
5 Australian gardens bloom in October.   T / F

2 Circle and read.

sunsnowhotfoggychillymildwarmrain

1 Pupils read the sentences and circle T (*true*) or F (*false*).
2 Pupils circle the words and read them aloud.

June, July and August are winter months in Australia. It's chilly but it's warmer than winter in Europe. It snows in some places and people go skiing.

In Australia, spring is in September, October and November. The trees grow green and tall and the gardens bloom.

Class Project

Four seasons of the year

Work in four groups and make a poster about the four seasons. One pupil from each group talks about a season in English.

DVD Club

surprise

mushrooms

wild mushrooms

poisonous

fresh air

1 Watch and number.

2 Watch, write and read.

air   campfire   home   mushrooms   surprise

1 Sam is writing a story at _____ .

2 Becky's Polish friends pick _____ in the forest.

3 Becky's dad likes the fresh _____ and the rain.

4 Sam sometimes cooks food on a _____ .

5 Becky's dad has got a _____ for the children.

3 Watch and say.

1 Pupils watch the DVD and number the photos in the correct order.
2 Pupils watch the DVD again, complete the sentences with the correct words and read the sentences aloud.
3 Pupils watch the slideshows and repeat the words.

Review 6

1 **Write and read.**

> September   May   January   July

1 I love spring. I'm going away in _____ .

2 I love winter. I'm going away in _____ .

3 I love autumn. I'm going away in _____ .

4 I love summer. I'm going away in _____ .

2 **Write, listen and read.** (2/38)

1 Summer is _____ than spring.
   a hotter   **b** colder   **c** longer

2 Cheetahs are _____ than lions.
   a slower   **b** easier   **c** faster

3 Winter in Europe is _____ than winter in Australia.
   a warmer   **b** shorter   **c** colder

4 A flower is _____ than a seed.
   a bigger   **b** lower   **c** smaller

5 February is _____ than January.
   a shorter   **b** bigger   **c** longer

6 Giraffes are _____ than zebras.
   a taller   **b** lower   **c** smaller

3 **Listen and sing.** (2/39)

1 Pupils complete the sentences with the names of the months and read them aloud.
2 Pupils complete the sentences with the correct adjectives, listen to the recording to check their answers
   and read the sentences aloud.
3 Pupils listen to the song and sing all together.

I can! My favourite season

I can! 😊 😐 🙁

1 I understand sentences that I hear and I can write the numbers correctly. 2/40

2 I can describe pictures using full sentences.

3 I can read and understand sentences.

In winter, the days are shorter than in summer. ☐

Flowers and trees grow in spring and summer. ☐

In autumn, animals get ready for winter. ☐

4 I can write sentences.

1 in   the weather   What's   like   November?

☐

_____

2 than   Winter   colder   summer.   is

☐

_____

Let's travel

Today I'm sailing a boat.

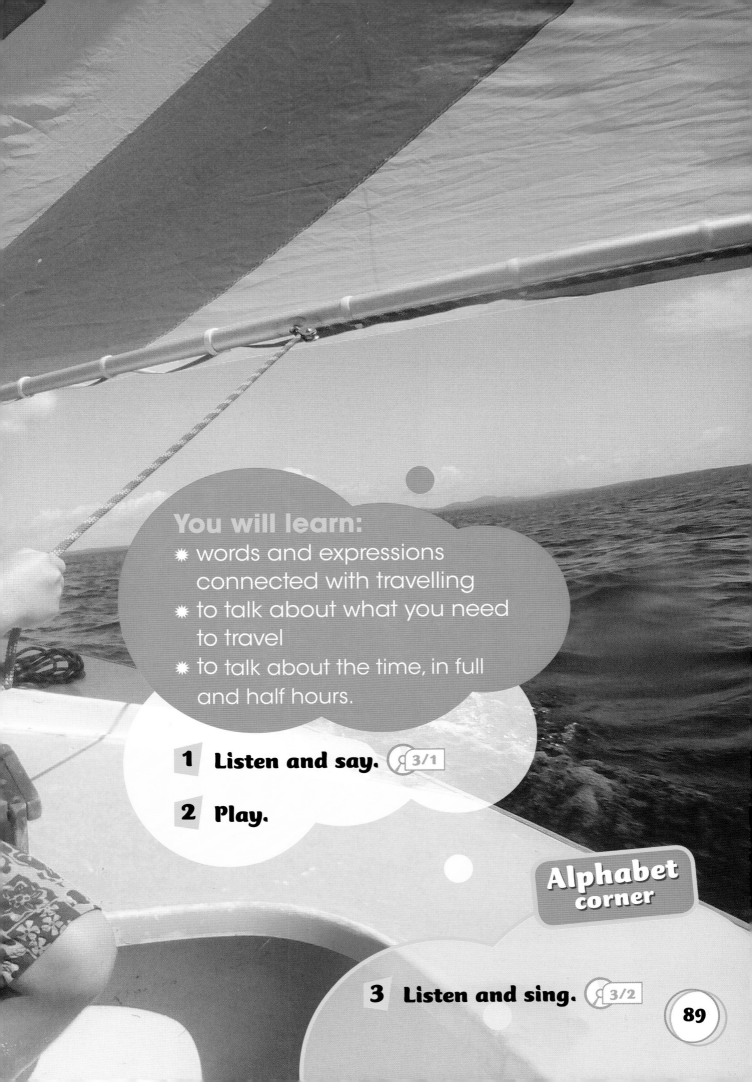

You will learn:
* words and expressions connected with travelling
* to talk about what you need to travel
* to talk about the time, in full and half hours.

1 Listen and say. 🎧 3/1

2 Play.

Alphabet corner

3 Listen and sing. 🎧 3/2

89

Where is Chatty?

Write the words and expressions in your language in the 'My language' column of the Word list at the end of the book.

Can you remember?   seaside   beach   suitcase
What time is it?   It's eleven o'clock.   go by bus
It's half past eleven.   take a taxi   airport   be late

1 Listen, say and play. 3/3

Story corner

2 Listen, read and make. 3/4

1 Pupils learn and say the new words and play the *Memory Game*. ⊃TB
2 Pupils listen to the dialogue, follow the story and read the sentences. ⊃TB

3 Match and read.

1

We're going away today.

2

I don't want to fly on a plane.

3

Are we going by bus?

4

We're going to the seaside!

5

What time is it?

4 Read and draw.

1 It's one o'clock.

2 It's eleven o'clock.

3 It's five o'clock.

4 It's half past nine.

5 It's half past eight.

6 It's half past ten.

5 Play.

Am I going to the mountains?

Yes, you are.

Am I flying on a plane?

No, you aren't. Try again!

MOUNTAINS TRAIN

3 Pupils match the characters with the correct sentences.
4 Pupils read the sentences and draw the correct time on the clock faces.
5 Pupils play the *Travel Game*. ⊃TB

91

Let's go to Egypt!

Write the words and expressions in your language in the 'My language' column of the Word list at the end of the book.

> desert   day   night   camel   river   holiday   sail on a boat   pyramid   hieroglyph

1 Listen, say and play. (3/5)

2 Listen and read. (3/6)

Egypt is in Africa. People like going on holiday to Egypt. There's a big desert, the Sahara. It is hot in the day and cold at night. You can ride a camel in the desert.

Egypt has got a very long river, the Nile. You can sail on a boat on the Nile. There are lots of beaches and some very old pyramids. You can see lots of hieroglyphs on their walls.

1 Pupils learn and say the new words, then play *Chinese Whispers*. ⤴TB
2 Pupils listen to the recording, follow the text and read it aloud.

3 Read and write.

1 Where is Egypt?

_____

2 Is the desert always hot?

_____

3 Is the Nile long?

_____

4 What is on the walls of the pyramids?

_____

4 Look, write and read.

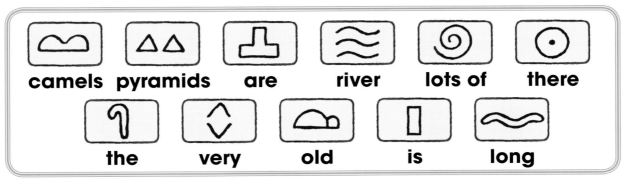

camels   pyramids   are   river   lots of   there

the   very   old   is   long

1 _____

2 _____

3 _____

5 Listen and sing. 3/7

3 Pupils read the questions and write down the answers.
4 In pairs, pupils decode the sentences, write them down and read them aloud.
5 Pupils listen to the song and sing it all together.

93

We must hurry!

Write the words and expressions in your language in the
'My language' column of the Word list at the end of the book.

> must   hurry   leave   backpack   camera   swimsuit
> map   ticket   money   passport

1 Listen, say and play. 3/8

2 Listen and read. 3/9

Mummy:	Where are you, Jane? We must hurry. We can't be late. Our train leaves at half past four.
Jane:	I'm waiting in the car, Mummy.
Mummy:	Have you got your backpack, Jane?
Jane:	Yes, I have. I've got my camera, my phone, my swimsuit, my hat, my book and a bottle of water.
Mummy:	Have you got the map?
Jane:	No, I haven't. It's in your bag.
Mummy:	It's four o'clock. Let's go!

Jane:	Mummy, have you got the tickets, the money and our passports?
Mummy:	What? Oh no! I haven't got my bag. It's at home!
Jane:	Well, let's go back and get it. We must hurry!

1 Pupils learn and say the new words and play *Sentence String*. ⊖TB
2 Pupils listen to the dialogue and read it aloud.

3 Look, write and say.

1 in Jane's backpack   **2** in Mummy's bag

Where is the camera?   It's in Jane's backpack.

4 Listen and chant. 3/10

5 Write and read.

When I travel I must have my _____ , my _____ ,

my _____ and my _____ in my _____ .

3 Pupils write the correct letters next to each photo and say the sentences.
4 Pupils listen to the chant and chant all together.
5 Pupils write about themselves and read the sentences aloud.

Wonderful world

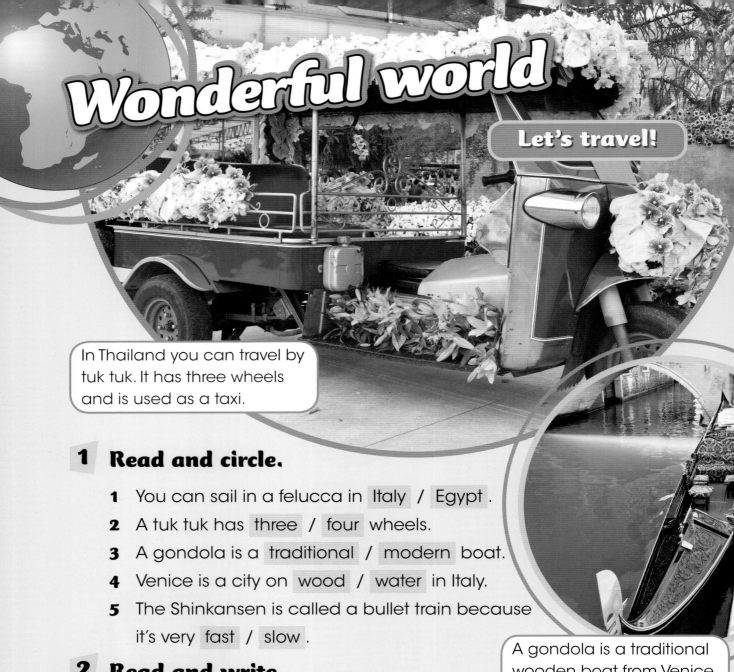

In Thailand you can travel by tuk tuk. It has three wheels and is used as a taxi.

A gondola is a traditional wooden boat from Venice, a city on water in Italy.

1 Read and circle.

1 You can sail in a felucca in Italy / Egypt .

2 A tuk tuk has three / four wheels.

3 A gondola is a traditional / modern boat.

4 Venice is a city on wood / water in Italy.

5 The Shinkansen is called a bullet train because it's very fast / slow .

2 Read and write.

bike boat bus car felucca
gondola plane taxi train tuk tuk

Land	Water	Air

1 Pupils read the sentences and circle the correct words.
2 Pupils read the words and write them in the correct columns.

Feluccas are sailing boats which are used on the Nile, in Egypt. They are very popular with tourists.

The Shinkansen is a high-speed train from Japan. It's sometimes called a bullet train.

Class Project

Eco-vehicle

Work in three groups and make vehicles on land, water or in the air. Then show your vehicle to the class and talk about it in English.

Pupils do a class project.

DVD Club

camping

Mexico City

expensive

appointment

WEDNESDAY
216

— 10 a.m. Doctor's

Priorities:

THURSDAY

tourists

1 Watch, tick and say.

1

2

3

4

5

6

2 Watch, circle and read.

1 Becky wants / doesn't want to go to Mexico.

2 Becky's dad thinks a holiday in Mexico is exciting / expensive .

3 Becky's dad wants to go camping / climbing .

4 Becky and her dad are late for the vet / doctor .

5 They need to take a bus / taxi because they are late.

3 Watch and say.

1 Pupils watch the DVD and tick the items they see.
2 Pupils watch the DVD again, circle the correct words and read the sentences aloud.
3 Pupils watch the slideshows and repeat the words.

Review **7**

1 Listen, stick and say. 3/11

1    2    3

4    5    6

2 Write and read.

> country   leaves   camera   backpacks   late
> ride   taxi   o'clock   see

My family is going on holiday to Egypt today. We've got two suitcases and two

_____ . We're taking a _____ to the airport. We can't be

_____ . Our plane _____ at five _____ .

I'd like to _____ a camel in the desert. My dad wants to

_____ the pyramids. My mum wants to take lots of photos so she's

got a _____ in the suitcase. Egypt is a hot _____ .

I'm happy we're going on holiday!

3 Listen and chant. 3/12

1 Pupils listen to the recording and stick the stickers in the correct places.
2 Pupils complete the sentences with the phrases from the box and read the text aloud.
3 Pupils listen to the chant and chant all together. ⊃TB

 **Let's travel.**

I can!

1 I understand sentences that I hear and I can write the numbers correctly. 3/13

2 I can describe a picture using full sentences.

3 I can read and understand sentences.

We must hurry.

Our bus leaves at half past nine.

I like flying on a plane but my brother likes sailing.

4 I can write sentences.

1   a taxi.   take   Let's

_____

2   your   you   got   backpack?   Have

_____

Our class

PE is our favourite school subject.

You will learn:
* the names of some school subjects
* to talk about your school trip
* to talk about your plans.

1 Listen and say. *3/14*

2 Listen and say *True* or *False*. *3/15*

Alphabet corner

3 **Listen and sing.** 🎧3/16

103

It's holiday time!

Write the words and expressions in your language in the 'My language' column of the Word list at the end of the book.

> end   report   mark   prize
> art   maths   IT   English   science   PE

1 Listen, say and play. 3/17

2 Listen, read and make. 3/18

Story corner

1 Pupils learn and say the new words and play *Find Your Pair*. ⊃TB
2 Pupils listen to the dialogue, follow the story and read the sentences. ⊃TB

3 Write and read.

maths art IT science PE English

1 Kate likes _____ , _____ , _____ , and

_____ .

2 Fred likes _____ and _____ .

3 Fred doesn't like _____ .

4 Listen, number and chant. 3/19

5 Write and read.

My timetable				
Monday	**Tuesday**	**Wednesday**	**Thursday**	**Friday**

3 Pupils write down the subjects which Fred and Kate like and don't like.
4 Pupils listen to the chant, number the pictures and chant all together.
5 Pupils write out their timetables and read them aloud.

A school trip

Write the words and expressions in your language in the 'My language' column of the Word list at the end of the book.

school trip   in the countryside   learn   tell us   ask a question
smell   herb   ant   butterfly/butterflies   outdoor game

1 **Listen, say and play.** 3/20

2 **Listen and read.** 3/21

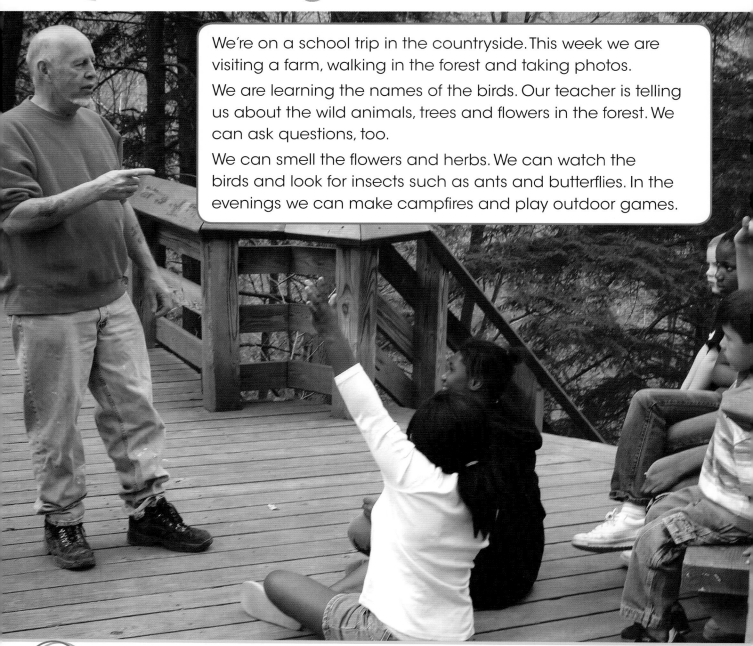

We're on a school trip in the countryside. This week we are visiting a farm, walking in the forest and taking photos.

We are learning the names of the birds. Our teacher is telling us about the wild animals, trees and flowers in the forest. We can ask questions, too.

We can smell the flowers and herbs. We can watch the birds and look for insects such as ants and butterflies. In the evenings we can make campfires and play outdoor games.

1 Pupils learn and say the new words, then play the *Echo Game*. ⏎TB
2 Pupils listen to the recording, follow the text and read it aloud.

3 Stick and read.

1 We are visiting   .

2 We are walking   .

3 We can smell   .

4 We can watch   .

5 We can make   .

6 We can play   .

4 Listen and sing. 3/22

5 Write and read.

1

in   the countryside.   are   We   walking

_____

2

can   watch   We   the wild animals.

_____

_____

3

a farm.   This   visiting   we   are   week

_____

3 Pupils stick the stickers in the correct places and read the sentences aloud.
4 Pupils listen to the song and sing all together.
5 Pupils write down the words in the correct order and read the sentences aloud.

School leaving party

Write the words and expressions in your language in the 'My language' column of the Word list at the end of the book.

> tomorrow   school leaving party   ballet performance   show
> amazing   train   twice a week   forget   invitation   bring   snack

1 Listen, say and play. 3/23

2 Listen and read. 3/24

Ms Barns: Listen, everybody. What's happening tomorrow? Can you remember?
Children: It's our school leaving party.
Ms Barns: That's right! What is everybody doing?

Judy: We're doing a ballet performance. Can we do it now?
Ms Barns: Yes, of course. Oh, that's beautiful.

Luke: We're doing a karate show. Come on boys!
Ms Barns: That's amazing. How often do you train?
Luke: We train twice a week, on Mondays and Thursdays.

Josh: I'm giving a short violin concert.
Ms Barns: You're a great musician, Josh. Can you play any other instruments?
Josh: No, I can't. I'd like to learn to play the trumpet.
Ms Barns: Don't forget the invitations for your parents and remember to bring some snacks and drinks! See you tomorrow!
Children: See you!

1 Pupils learn and say the new words and play the *Memory Game*. ⏎TB
2 Pupils listen to the dialogue and read it aloud.

3 Circle and read.

At the school leaving party tomorrow the children are:

singing

doing karate

making pizzas

dancing

doing their homework

giving a concert

baking gingerbread cookies

bringing snacks and drinks to school

making campfires

4 Listen and sing. 3/25

5 Write and read.

1 Tomorrow morning I am _____ .

2 Tomorrow evening I am _____ .

3 Next summer I am _____ .

3 Pupils circle the correct phrases and read the sentences aloud.
4 Pupils listen to the song and sing all together.
5 Pupils complete the sentences about themselves and read them aloud.

Wonderful world

Nursery school is for young children aged three and four years old. The children enjoy playing and learning. They have a lot of fun.

In primary school, pupils aged from five to ten years old study many different subjects, such as English, maths, science and PE.

1 Read and match.

Nursery school	from 11 to 16 or 18 years old
Primary school	3 and 4 year olds
Secondary school	after 18
College or university	from 5 to 10 years old

2 Read and circle.

1 learn	play	have fun	job
2 science	school	maths	chemistry
3 college	nursery school	biology	primary school
4 pupils	subjects	children	students

1 Pupils match the types of schools to the ages of the students who attend.
2 Pupils circle the odd one out in each line.

Secondary school is for children aged from eleven to sixteen or eighteen years old. Children learn many new subjects in secondary school, such as biology, chemistry and IT.

College or university prepares students for jobs in the future. Oxford University and Cambridge University are famous.

Class Project

Class diary

Make a class diary, where you gather information about pupils, important events and descriptions of class trips. Describe interesting class events in English.

OUR SCHOOL TRIP

OUR CAMPSITE

OUTDOOR GAME

HERE WE ARE!

Sylvia
Jim
Matthew
Allen
Sam
Maria
Jessica
Lucy
Peter
John
Joe
Tom

goats

feeding

rehearsal

stroke

1 Watch and match.

animals  farm park

prizes reports

school play  school trip

2 Watch, circle and say.

The goats are …

young

big	old
hungry	sweet
ill	tired
naughty	young

3 Watch and say.

Goodbye!

1 Pupils watch the DVD and match the words to the characters.
2 Pupils watch the DVD again, circle the correct words and describe the goats.
3 Pupils watch the slideshows and repeat the words.

Review 8

1 Listen and write. 3/26

1 Look at these insects! This is a butterfly and this is an _____ .

2 Do you like playing _____ games?

3 This week, we are _____ a farm and walking in the forest.

4 In the evenings we can make a _____ .

2 Circle and write.

maths	r	e	p	o	r	t	a	r	c	f
English	t	e	a	c	h	e	r	g	g	i
art	h	u	b	s	u	b	j	e	c	t
science	j	a	r	t	j	a	m	a	r	k
subject	l	s	h	o	l	i	d	a	y	s
teacher	t	e	s	c	i	e	n	c	e	s
holiday	h	a	e	n	g	l	i	s	h	s
mark	m	a	t	h	s	p	p	y	n	e
report										

_____

_____

_____

_____

_____

_____

_____

_____

3 Talk.

What are you doing tomorrow evening?

I'm playing computer games.

1 Pupils listen to the recording and write down the missing words. Then they read the sentences aloud.
2 Pupils find and circle the hidden words in the puzzle and write them on the lines.
3 Pupils do a class survey and report their findings to the class.

 **Our class**

I can! 😊 😐 ☹

1 I understand sentences that I hear and I can write the numbers correctly. 3/27

2 I can describe a picture using full sentences.

3 I can read and understand sentences.

What is your favourite school subject? ☐

Outdoor lessons and school trips are fun! ☐

Tomorrow we are having a school leaving party. ☐

4 I can write sentences.

1 reading.   I've   for   got   a prize

_____ ☐

2 watch   the birds   I   the countryside.   always   in

_____ ☐

Halloween

Write the words and expressions in your language in the 'My language' column of the Word list at the end of the book.

> Trick or treat!   costume   witch   pink
> skeleton   ghost   vampire

1 Listen, say and play. 3/28

2 Listen and read. 3/29

Sam:	Hello, Mrs Barclay. Trick or treat!
Mrs Barclay:	You're all good children so here's a treat for everybody.
Emma:	Thanks. Yummy! Do you like my blue costume? I'm a witch.
Mrs Barclay:	It's a great costume.
Rosie:	I'm a pink witch. I've got a bag too. It's a pumpkin.
Matt:	I'm a skeleton. I'm wearing a scary mask!
Mrs Barclay:	Your costumes are great! Are there any ghosts or vampires?
Sam:	I'm a vampire! But there aren't any ghosts this year.
Mrs Barclay:	Goodbye, children. Happy Halloween!
Children:	Goodbye, Mrs Barclay. Happy Halloween!

3 Make, listen and sing. 3/30

1 Pupils learn and say the new words, then play *Call Out*. ⊃TB
2 Pupils listen to the recording, follow the text and read it aloud.
3 Pupils cut out the puppets, listen to the Halloween song and sing all together. ⊃TB

Valentine's Day

Write the words and expressions in your language in the 'My language' column of the Word list at the end of the book.

> lovely   rose   ring   perfume   card   heart
> inside   I love you!

1 Listen, say and play. 3/31

2 Listen and read. 3/32

Tom:	Tomorrow is February 14th. It's Valentine's Day. Daddy has got these lovely presents for Mummy.
Hannah:	Look at this beautiful red rose. What's in the box?
Tom:	I think it's some chocolates. Mummy likes chocolates.
Hannah:	Or maybe it's a ring or some perfume.
Tom:	No, I think it's chocolates. Has Mummy got a present for Daddy?
Hannah:	Yes, she has got a card for him. It's a red heart. Inside the card it says 'I love you.'
Tom:	That's nice.

3 Make and write.

4 Listen and sing. 3/33

1 Pupils learn and say the new words, then play *Sentence String*. ⊃TB
2 Pupils listen to the recording, follow the text and read it aloud.
3 Pupils make a Valentine's card.
4 Pupils listen to a Valentine's Day song and sing all together.

117

Play Aladdin

Write the words and expressions in your language in the 'My language' column of the Word list at the end of the book.

> princess   poor   That's good news!   gold   magician
> Don't leave me …   cave   bad man   dirty   clean   wish
> master   free

1 Listen and say. 3/34

2 Listen, read and make. 3/35

1
I love Princess Jasmine, but I'm poor.

There's Aladdin.

2
Hello. I'm your uncle.

That's good news!

3
I have got the gold now! Ha, ha!

Don't leave me in this cave.

4
This lamp is dirty. I can clean it. What's happening?

1 Pupils learn and say the new words. ◌TB
2 Pupils listen to the dialogue, follow the story and read the sentences. ◌TB

3 Play.

The Alphabet Song

A and B and C and D
I like you and you like me.
D and C and B and A
Come with me. Let's play.

E and F and G and H
Look at this page! H
H and G and F and E
Now, look at me! E

I and J and K and L
Stand up and ring the bell.
L and K and J and I
Jump three times and say goodbye.
GOODBYE!

M and N and O and P
Turn around and count to three.
P and O and N and M
Clap your hands and say jam.
JAM!

Q and R and S and T
Stamp your feet and look at me.
T and S and R and Q
Let's play: me and you.

U and V and W
Do you like the colour blue?
W and V and U
I like blue and you?

X and Y and last is Z
I prefer the colour red.
Z and Y and also X
Which letter is next?

We know all the letters now.
Let's take a bow.

Word list

Unit 1   My language

baking
collect
cookie
do karate
favourite
gardening
Help!
hiking
leaf/leaves
Let me …
live
Me too!
play the piano
poster
ride a horse
soft toy
stamp
take a photo
travelling
write a
story/stories

thirty
forty
fifty
sixty
seventy
eighty
ninety
one hundred

Unit 2   My language

beautiful
biggest
bird
cheetah
dangerous
difficult
egg
elephant
forest
fox
gentle
giraffe
hummingbird
hunt
I don't know.
miss
I think …
insect
land animal
Let's go home.
lion
mouse/mice
neck
ostrich
question
see
smallest
stripe
tall
zebra

Unit ③   My language

chef
doctor
drive
exciting
fire engine
firefighter
fly
Here you are.
hospital
hungry
important
kitten
letter
medicine
need
nurse
parcel
pilot
postman
restaurant
touch
treat
vet
waiter
work

Unit ④   My language

add
bake
bowl
butter
carrot
chicken
chocolate
cake
cup
delicious
Enjoy your meal.
farmer
fish and chips
flour
ginger
glass of milk
grow
Help yourself.
lettuce
lettuces
menu
mix
one more
potato
pumpkin
put
shop assistant
sugar
teaspoon
tomato soup
vegetables
village

Word list

Unit 5 — My language

bored
brush
brush teeth
busy
difficult
early
easy
evening
flute
get dressed
get washed
give a concert
have breakfast
have dinner
I'd like to sleep late.
I'd like to stay up late.
I'm sorry.
later
morning
musician
paint
timetable
together
violin
wake up
week

Monday
Tuesday
Wednesday
Thursday
Friday
Saturday
Sunday

Unit 6 — My language

autumn
campfire
get ready
go away
go for a walk
highest
learn
lower
month
mountain
next year
plant
sausage
seed
skier
spring
sunflower
toast
wait
warm

January
February
March
April
May
June
July
August
September
October
November
December

Unit (7) My language

airport
backpack
be late
beach
camel
camera
Can you remember?
day
desert
go by bus
hieroglyph
holiday
hurry
It's eleven o'clock.
It's half past eleven.
leave
map
money
must
night
passport
pyramid
river
sail on a boat
seaside
suitcase
swimsuit
take a taxi
ticket
What time is it?

Unit (8) My language

amazing
ant
art
ask a question
ballet performance
bring
butterfly/ butterflies
end
English
forget
herb
in the countryside
invitation
IT
mark
maths
outdoor game
PE
prize
report
school leaving party
school trip
science
show
smell
snack
tell us
tomorrow
train
twice a week

Word list

Celebrations – Halloween

costume
ghost
pink
skeleton
Trick or treat!
vampire
witch

Celebrations – Valentine's Day

card
heart
I love you!
inside
lovely
perfume
ring
rose

Play	My language
bad man	
cave	
clean	
dirty	
Don't leave me.	
free	
gold	
magician	
master	
poor	
princess	
That's good news!	
wish	

Hopscotch Pupil's Book 3

Jennifer Heath

Publisher: Gavin McLean

Editorial Manager: Claire Merchant

Project Manager: Dorothy Robertson

Editor: Carole Hughes

Head of Production: Celia Jones

Art Director cover: Alex von Dallwitz

Senior Designer cover: Cari Wynkoop

Compositor: MPS Limited

Audio Producer: Liz Hammond

Acknowledgements:

Audio recorded at Motivation Sound Studios and GFS-PRO Studio.

Music composed by Evdoxia Banani and Vagelis Markontonis

Production at GFS-PRO Studio by George Flamouridis

© 2016 National Geographic Learning, as part of Cengage Learning

ALL RIGHTS RESERVED. No part of this work covered by the copyright herein may be reproduced, transmitted, stored or used in any form or by any means graphic, electronic, or mechanical, including but not limited to photocopying, recording, scanning, digitising, taping, Web distribution, information networks, or information storage and retrieval systems, except as permitted under Section 107 or 108 of the 1976 United States Copyright Act, or applicable copyright law of another jurisdiction, without the prior written permission of the publisher.

For permission to use material from this text or product, submit all requests online at **cengage.com/permissions**

Further permissions questions can be emailed to **permissionrequest@cengage.com.**

ISBN: 978-1-4080-9713-7

National Geographic Learning

Cheriton House, North Way, Andover, Hampshire, SP10 5BE United Kingdom

Cengage Learning is a leading provider of customised learning solutions with office locations around the globe, including Singapore, the United Kingdom, Australia, Mexico, Brazil and Japan. Locate our local office at **international.cengage.com/region**

Cengage Learning products are represented in Canada by Nelson Education Ltd.

Visit National Geographic Learning online at **ngl.cengage.com**
Visit our corporate website at **www.cengage.com**

Cover photo: (Stuart Westmorland/The Image Bank/Getty Images)

Inside photos: pp 1 b (Joel Sartore/National Geographic Creative), 14 bl (Zooid Pictures), 15 mr (Zooid Pictures), 18-19 (Robin Moore/National Geographic Creative), 29 (Zooid Pictures), 36 (Amy White & Al Petteway/National Geographic Creative), 43 br (Zooid Pictures), 46-47 (Richard Nowitz/National Geographic Creative), 57 tm, mm, bm (Zooid Pictures), 60-61 (Jack Hollingsworth/Getty Images), 64 (Rich Reid/National Geographic Creative), 71 (Zooid Pictures), 85 tl, tr, ml, mr, bl (Zooid Pictures), 88-89 (Skip Brown/National Geographic Creative), 92 (Martin Gray/National Geographic Creative), 95 j (Eddie Gerald/Alamy), 101 f (Eddie Gerald/Alamy), 111 bl (Patrick Wittmann/Cultura/Getty Images), 111 br (Caiaimage/Paul Bradbury Ojo+/Getty Images), 113 t, tm, b (Zooid Pictures)

Shutterstock:
1 t, mr, ml, 2, 3, 4-5, 8, 10, 12, 13, 14 tl, tr, bkgd, ml, br, 15 br, tr, ml, bl, tl, 16, 17, 21, 22, 24, 26, 27, 28, 30, 31, 32-33, 38, 39, 40, 41, 42, 43 m, bl, 44, 45, 50, 52, 53, 54, 55, 56, 57, 58, 59, 66, 67, 68, 69, 70, 71 tl, ml, 72, 73, 74-75, 78, 80, 82, 83, 84, 85 br, 86, 87, 94, 95 a, b, c, d, e, f, g, h, i, 96, 97, 98, 99, 100, 101 a, b, c, d, e, g, 102-103, 106, 108, 110, 111 l, r, m, 112, 113 bm, 114, 115, 116, 117, 121, 123, 125

Printed in China by RR Donnelley
Print Number 01   Print Year 2015

Unit 1, page 7

I ride my horse.

I do karate.

I take photos.

I write stories.

I play the piano.

Unit 1, page 16

Unit 2, page 25

Unit 3, page 39

flies

parcels

pilot

firefighter

letters

fire engine

Unit 4, page 53

butter

teaspoon

one cup

flour

eggs

Unit 4, page 58

Unit 5, page 67

get washed	play computer games	wake up early
have dinner	have breakfast	brush their teeth
go to bed early	have breakfast in bed	stay up late

Unit 6, page 81

Unit 7, page 100

Unit 8, page 107

the flowers	the birds	campfires
outdoor games	a farm	in the forest